Somebody Loves You

HELEN STEINER RICE

Somebody Loves You

Fleming H. Revell Company
Tarrytown, New York

Library of Congress Cataloging in Publication Data
Rice, Helen Steiner.
  Somebody loves you.

  1. Christian poetry, American.   I. Title.
PS3568.I28S58   811'.5'4   76-25559
ISBN 0-8007-1670-1

Contents

The Helen Steiner Rice Foundation

Whatever the celebration, whatever the day, whatever the event, whatever the occasion, Helen Steiner Rice possessed the ability to express the appropriate feeling for that particular moment in time.

A happening became happier, a sentiment more sentimental, a memory more memorable because of her deep sensitivity to put into understandable language the emotion being experienced. Her positive attitude, her concern for others, and her love of God are identifiable threads woven into her life, her works . . . and even her death.

Prior to her passing, she established the HELEN STEINER RICE FOUNDATION, a nonprofit corporation whose purpose is to award grants to worthy charitable programs that aid the elderly, the needy, and the poor. In her lifetime, these were the individuals about whom Mrs. Rice was greatly concerned.

Royalties from the sale of this book will add to the financial capabilities of the HELEN STEINER RICE FOUNDATION, thus making possible additional grants to various qualified, worthwhile, and charitable programs. Because of her foresight, her caring, and her deep convictions, Helen Steiner Rice continues to touch a countless number of lives. Thank you for your assistance in helping to keep Helen's dream alive.

Virginia J. Ruehlmann, Administrator
The Helen Steiner Rice Foundation
Suite 2100, Atrium Two
221 E. Fourth Street
Cincinnati, Ohio 45202

Introduction

God loves you and He loves me, too.
And through His love I share with you.
For my work is a partnership of three—
God first, then you, and last of all me.

Helen Steiner Rice

Somebody Loves You

Somebody Loves You

Somebody Loves You

Somebody loves you more than you know,
Somebody goes with you wherever you go,
Somebody really and truly cares
And lovingly listens to all of your prayers.

Don't doubt for a minute
      that this is true,
For God loves His children
      and takes care of them, too.

God's Love

God's love is like an island
In life's ocean vast and wide,
A peaceful, quiet shelter
From the restless, rising tide.

God's love is like an anchor
When the angry billows roll,
A mooring in the storms of life,
A stronghold for the soul.

God's love is like a fortress
And we seek protection there
When the waves of tribulation
Seem to drown us in despair.

God's love is like a harbor
Where our souls can find sweet rest
From the struggle and the tension
Of life's fast and futile quest.

He Loves You

It's amazing and incredible,
But it's as true as it can be,
God loves and understands us all
And that means you and me.

His love knows no exceptions,
So never feel excluded,
No matter who or what you are
Your name has been included.

And no matter what your past has been,
Trust God to understand,
And no matter what your problem is
Just place it in His hand.

For in all of our unloveliness
This great God loves us still,
He loved us since the world began
And what's more, He always will!

Enfolded in His Love

The love of God surrounds us
Like the air we breathe around us—
As near as a heartbeat,
      as close as a prayer,
And whenever we need Him
      He'll always be there!

One Thing Never Changes

The seasons swiftly come and go
And with them comes the thought
Of all the various changes
That time in flight has brought.

But one thing never changes,
It remains the same forever,
God truly loves His children
And He will forsake them never!

My God Is No Stranger

God is no stranger
      in a faraway place,
He's as close as the wind
      that blows 'cross my face.
The sky and the stars,
      the waves and the sea,
The dew on the grass,
      the leaves on a tree
Are constant reminders of God
      and His nearness,
Proclaiming His presence
      with crystal-like clearness.
So how could I think
      God was far, far away
When I feel Him beside me
      every hour of the day?

Wondrous Evidence

Who can see the dawn break through
  without a glimpse of heaven
  and You.
For who but God could make the day
  and gently put the night away.

Put Your Problem in
God's Hands

Although it sometimes seems to us
      our prayers have not been heard,
God always knows our every need
      without a single word.

And He will not forsake us
      even though the way seems steep,
For always He is near to us
      a tender watch to keep.

In good time He will answer us
      and in His love He'll send
Greater things than we have asked
      and blessings without end.

So though we do not understand
      why trouble comes to man
Can we not be contented
      just to know that it's God's plan?

"Seek Ye First the Kingdom of God"

Always remember
      that whatever betide you
The power of God
      is always beside you,
And if friends disappoint you
      and plans go astray
And nothing works out
      in just the right way
And you feel you have failed
      in achieving your goal
And that life wrongly placed you
      in an unfitting role,
Take heart and stand tall
      and think who you are,

For God is your Father
       and no one can bar
Or keep you from reaching
       your desired success
Or withhold the joy
       that is yours to possess.
For with God on your side
       it matters not who
Is working to keep
       life's good things from you.
So trust in His wisdom
       and follow His ways
And be not concerned
       with the world's empty praise,
But seek first His Kingdom
       and you will possess
The world's greatest riches
       which is true happiness.

God's Assurance Gives Us Endurance

My blessings are so many,
My troubles are so few,
How can I feel discouraged
When I know that I have You
And I have the sweet assurance
That I'll never stand alone
If I but keep remembering
I am Yours and Yours alone.

So, in this world of trouble
With darkness all around,
Take my hand and lead me
Until I stand on higher ground
And help me to endure the storms
That keep raging deep inside me
And make me more aware each day
That no evil can betide me
If I remain undaunted
Though the billows sweep and roll,
Knowing I have Your assurance
There's a haven for my soul.

For anything and everything
Can somehow be endured
If Your presence is beside me
And lovingly assured!

The Reflections of God

The silent stars in timeless skies,
The wonderment in children's eyes,
The autumn haze, the breath of spring,
The chirping song the crickets sing,
A rosebud in a slender vase
Are all reflections of God's face.

Faith Is the Key to Heaven

O Father, grant once more to men
A simple, childlike faith again,
Forgetting color, race, and creed
And seeing only the heart's deep need.

For faith alone can save man's soul
And lead him to a higher goal,
For there's but one unfailing course—
We win by faith and not by force.

Live by Faith and Not by Feelings

When everything is pleasant and bright
And the things we do turn out just right,
We know without question that God is real,
For, when we are happy, how good we feel.

But when the tides turn and gone is the song
And misfortune comes and our plans go wrong,
Doubt creeps in and we start to wonder
And our thoughts about God are torn asunder.

For we feel deserted in time of deep stress,
Without God's presence to assure us and bless.
And it is then when our senses are reeling
We realize clearly it's faith and not feeling.

For it takes great faith to patiently wait,
Believing God comes not too soon or too late.

Trust Is a Must

"I have no faith," the skeptic cries,
"I can only accept what I see with my eyes."
Yet man has to have faith or he would never
        complete
Just a simple task like crossing the street,
For he has to have faith in his manly stride
To get him across to the other side,
And the world would be panic-stricken indeed
If no one thought that he could succeed
In doing the smallest, simplest thing
That life with its many demands can bring.
So why do the skeptics still ridicule
And call the man of faith a fool
When faith is the basis of all that we do,
And that includes unbelievers, too?

The Master Builder

God is the Master Builder,
His plans are perfect and true,
And when He sends you sorrow
It's part of His plan for you.

For all things work together
To complete the Master Plan
And God up in His heaven
Can see what's best for man.

Life Is a Highway

Life is a highway
      on which the years go by.
Sometimes the road is level,
      sometimes the hills are high.
But as we travel onward
      to a future that's unknown
We can make each mile we travel
      a heavenly stepping-stone!

"Love Divine,
All Loves Excelling"

In a myriad of miraculous ways
God shapes our lives and changes our days,
Beyond our will or even knowing
God keeps our spirit ever growing.

For lights and shadows, sun and rain,
Sadness and gladness, joy and pain
Combine to make our lives complete,
And give us victory through defeat.

"Oh, love divine, all loves excelling,"
In troubled hearts You just keep dwelling,
Patiently waiting for a prodigal son
To say at last, "Thy will be done."

A Time of Renewal and Spiritual Blessing

No one likes to be sick
      and yet we know
It takes sunshine and rain
      to make flowers grow.
And if we never were sick
      and never felt pain,
We'd be like a desert
      without any rain,
And who wants a life
      that is barren and dry
With never a cloud
      to darken the sky?
For continuous sun
      goes unrecognized
Like the blessings God sends
      which are often disguised,
For sometimes a sickness
      that seems so distressing
Is a time of renewal
      and a spiritual blessing.

Today, Tomorrow, and Always He Is There

In sickness or health,
In suffering and pain,
In storm-laden skies,
In sunshine and rain,
God is always there
To lighten your way
And lead you through darkness
To a much brighter day.

Be Not Dismayed
By Dismal Days

It's a dismal, dreary morning
       and as I sometimes do
I feel a little dreary
       and kinda downcast, too,
For let nobody tell you
       that life's a happy song
And that we just keep smiling
       when everything goes wrong.

For it just would not be natural
       to always wear a smile.
A smile would be a silly grin
       if it covered up a trial.
For there are certain periods
       when the soul is sweetly sad
As it contemplates the mystery
       of both good times and bad.

We're not really discontented
and we are never unaware
That the good Lord up in heaven
has us always in His care,
But the soul of man is restless
and it just keeps longing for
A haven that is safe and sure
that will last forevermore.

And as I sit here writing this
a thought passed through my mind—
"Why dwell on past or future
or what's ahead or gone behind?"
Just follow God unquestioningly
because you love Him so,
For if you trust His judgment
there is nothing you need know!

Our Refuge and
Strength

The Lord is our salvation
And our strength in every fight,
Our Redeemer and Protector,
Our eternal guiding light.

He has promised to sustain us,
He's our refuge from all harms,
And underneath this refuge
Are the everlasting arms!

Are You Physically Ill or Soul Sick?

Sometimes when we are
          physically ill
We're prone to resort
          to a tonic or pill,
Neglecting to place
          ourselves in God's care
By seeking His help
          on the wings of prayer.
For God can remove
          our uncertain fear
And replace our worry
          with healing cheer.
So close your eyes
          and open your heart,
And let God come in
          and freely impart
A brighter outlook
          and new courage, too,
As His spiritual sunshine
          smiles on you.

We Never Walk Alone

What more can we ask of the Savior
Than to know we are never alone
That His mercy and love are unfailing
And He makes all our problems His own.

God's Tender Care

When trouble comes,
       as it does to us all,
God is so great
       and we are so small.
But there is nothing
       that we need know
If we have faith
       that wherever we go
God will be waiting
       to help us bear
Our pain and sorrow,
       our suffering and care.
For no pain or suffering
       is ever too much
To yield itself
       to God's merciful touch!

In God Is My Strength

"Love divine, all loves excelling"
Makes my humbled heart Your dwelling,
For without Your love divine
Total darkness would be mine.
My earthly load I could not bear
If You were not there to share
All the pain, despair, and sorrow
That almost makes me dread tomorrow.
For I am often weak and weary
And life is dark and bleak and dreary,
But somehow when I realize
That He who made the sea and skies
And holds the whole world in His hand
Has my small soul in His command,
It gives me strength to try once more
To somehow reach the heavenly door
Where I will live forevermore
With friends and loved ones I adore!

In God We Are Secure

Faith makes it wholly possible
        to quietly endure
The violent world around us
        for in God we are secure.

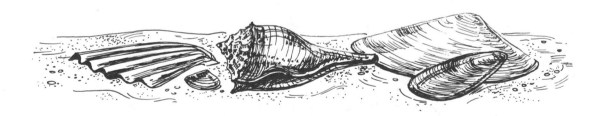

God's Presence Is Ever Beside You

And so today I walk with God
Because I love Him so,
If I have faith and trust in Him,
There's nothing I need know!

God's Hand Is Always There

I am perplexed and often vexed
And sometimes I cry and sadly sigh,
But do not think, Dear Father above,
I question You or Your unchanging love.

It's just sometimes when I reach out
You seem to be nowhere about . . .
And while I'm sure that You love me still
And I know in my heart that You always will,

Somehow I feel that I cannot reach You
And though I get down on my knees and
                beseech You,
I cannot bring You closer to me
And I feel adrift on life's raging sea.

But though I cannot find Your hand
To lead me on to the Promised Land,
I still believe with all my being
Your hand is there beyond my seeing!

People's Problems

Everyone has problems
        in this restless world of care,
Everyone grows weary
        with the cross they have to bear,
Everyone is troubled
        and their skies are overcast
As they try to face the future
        while still dwelling in the past.

But the people with their problems
        only listen with one ear
For people only listen
        to the things they want to hear
And they only hear the kind of things
        they are able to believe
And the answers that are God's to give
        they're not ready to receive,

So while the people's problems
        keep growing every day
And man vainly tries to solve them
        in his own self-willful way
God seeks to help and watches,
        waiting always patiently
To help them solve their problems
        whatever they may be.

So may the people of all nations
        at last become aware
That God will solve the people's problems
        through faith and hope and prayer!

This Is Just a Resting Place

Sometimes the road of life seems long
    as we travel through the years
And, with a heart that's broken
    and eyes brimful of tears,
We falter in our weariness
    and sink beside the way,
But God leans down and whispers,
    "Child, there'll be another day."
And the road will grow much smoother
    and much easier to face,
So do not be disheartened—
    this is just a resting place.

The Mystery and Miracle of His Creative Hand

In the beauty of a snowflake,
Falling softly on the land,
Is the mystery and the miracle
Of God's great, creative hand!

How Little We Know of
Suffering and Woe

God, how little I was really aware
Of the pain and the trouble and deep despair
That floods the hearts of those in pain
As they struggle to cope but feel it's in vain,
Crushed with frustration and with no haven to seek,
With broken spirits and bodies so weak.

And yet they forget Christ suffered and died
And hung on the cross and was crucified,
And He did it all so some happy day,
When the sorrows of earth have all passed away,
We who have suffered will forever be free
To live with God in eternity!

Put Your Soul in
God's Control

Many trials and troubles
Are scattered on our way,
Daily little crosses
Are a part of every day.

But the troubles we have suffered
Are over, passed, and through,
So why should bygone happenings
Keep on gravely troubling you?

For the problems that beset us
In the now and present hour
We need not try to solve alone
Without God's grace and power.

And those scheduled for tomorrow
Still belong to God alone,
They are still unborn and formless
And a part of the unknown.

So let us face the trouble
That is ours this present minute
And count on God to help us
And put His mercy in it.

And forget the past and future
And dwell wholly on today,
For God controls the future
And He will direct our way.

My Daily Prayer

God, be my resting place and my protection
In hours of trouble, defeat, and dejection.
May I never give way to self-pity and sorrow,
May I always be sure of a better tomorrow,
May I stand undaunted come what may
Secure in the knowledge I have only to pray
And ask my Creator and Father above
To keep me serene in His grace and His love!

Build a Firm Foundation of Faith

Build a Firm
Foundation of Faith

Faith is a force that is greater
Than knowledge or power or skill,
And the darkest defeat turns to triumph
If we trust in God's wisdom and will.

Trust and Believe

Whatever our problems, troubles, and sorrows,
If we trust in the Lord, there'll be brighter
       tomorrows,
For there's nothing too much for the Great God
       to do,
And all that He asks or expects from you
Is faith that's unshaken by tribulations and tears
That keeps growing stronger along with the years,
Content in the knowledge that God knows best
And that trouble and sorrow are only a test,
For without God's testing of our soul
It never would reach its ultimate goal.
So keep on believing, whatever betide you,
Knowing that God will be with you to guide you.

He Answers All
Our Needs

There's no problem too big
      and no question too small,
Just ask God in faith
      and He'll answer them all.
Not always at once,
      so be patient and wait,
For God never comes
      too soon or too late
So trust in His wisdom
      and believe in His Word,
For no prayer's unanswered
      and no prayer's unheard.

If We but Believe

If we put our problems in God's hand,
There is nothing we need understand . . .
It is enough to just believe
That what we need we will receive.

With God All Things Are Possible

Nothing is ever too hard to do
If your faith is strong and your purpose is true,
So never give up and never stop,
Just journey on to the mountaintop!

New Life and Joy

The flowers sleeping peacefully
Beneath the winter's snow
Awaken from their icy grave
When spring winds start to blow.

And little brooks and singing streams,
Icebound beneath the snow,
Begin to babble merrily
Beneath the sun's warm glow.

And all around on every side
New life and joy appear
To tell us nothing ever dies
And we should have no fear,

For death is just a detour
Along life's wending way
That leads God's chosen children
To a bright and glorious day.

Help Us to See and Understand

God, give us wider vision
      to see and understand
That both the sun and showers
      are gifts from Thy great hand,
And when our lives are overcast
      with trouble and with care,
Give us faith to see beyond
      the dark clouds of despair,
And give us strength to rise above
      the mist of doubt and fear
And recognize the hidden smile
      behind each burning tear.
Teach us that it takes the showers
      to make the flowers grow
And only in the storms of life
      when the winds of trouble blow
Can man, too, reach maturity
      and grow in faith and grace
And gain the strength and courage
      to enable him to face
Sunny days as well as rain,
      high peaks as well as low,
Knowing that the April showers
      will make the May flowers grow.
And then at last may we accept
      the sunshine and the showers,
Confident it takes them both
      to make salvaton ours!

God, Grant Me . . .

Courage and hope
      for every day,
Faith to guide me
      along my way,
Understanding
      and wisdom, too,
And grace to accept
      what life gives me to do.

Sorrow Helps Our Souls to Grow

There's a lot of comfort in the thought
That sorrow, grief, and woe
Are sent into our lives sometimes
To help our souls to grow.

For through the depths of sorrow
Comes understanding love,
And peace and truth and comfort
Are sent from God above.

Learn to Recognize
a Blessing

While it's very difficult
      for mankind to understand
God's intentions and His purpose
      and the workings of His hand,
If we observe the miracles
      that happen every day,
We cannot help but be convinced
      that in His wondrous way
God makes what seemed unbearable
      and painful and distressing
Easily acceptable
      when we view it as a blessing.

We Can't Have a Crown Without a Cross

We all have those days
        that are dismal and dreary
And we feel sorta blue
        and lonely and weary,
But we have to admit
        that life is worth living
And God gives us reasons
        for daily thanksgiving.
For life's an experience
        God's children go through
That's made up of gladness
        and much sadness, too.
But we have to know both
        the bitter and sweet
If we want a good life
        that is full and complete.
For each trial we suffer
        and every shed tear
Just gives us new strength
        to persevere
As we climb the steep hills
        along life's way
That lead us at last
        to that wonderful day
Where the cross we have carried
        becomes a crown
And at last we can lay
        our burden down!

To Really Live Is to Give and Forgive!

Since God forgives us,
        we, too, must forgive
And resolve to do better
        each day that we live
By constantly trying
        to be like Him more nearly
And to trust in His wisdom
        and love Him more dearly.

Tomorrow I'll Think About God

Not today when I am so busy,
Not today when there's so much to do,
Not today while I'm young and eager
And life is far-reaching and new,

But tomorrow when I am older
And the tempo of life is less,
I'll have more time for praying
And for meditating, I guess.

But time is swift in its passing
And before we are really aware
We find ourselves growing older
And daily in need of God's care.

And while God is always ready
To help us and lead us along,
Because we have tarried and wasted
Our young days in dancing and song,

We find we are not well acquainted
With the wonderful love of the Lord
And we feel very strange in His presence
And unworthy of our Father's reward—

For only the children who seek Him
With hearts yet untouched and still clean
Can ever experience His greatness
And know what His love can mean.

So waste not the hours of life's morning,
Get acquainted with God when you're born,
And when you come to life's evening,
It will shine like the glory of morn!

God's Mighty Handiwork

"The earth is the Lord's
      and the fulness thereof"
It speaks of His greatness
      and it sings of His love
It whispers of mysteries
      we cannot comprehend
Of a beautiful land
      where life has no end!

"Thy Will Be Done"

God did not promise sun without rain,
       light without darkness or joy without pain.
He only promised us strength for the day
       when the darkness comes and we lose our
       way,
For only through sorrow do we grow more aware
       that God is our refuge in times of despair.
For when we are happy and life's bright and fair,
       we often forget to kneel down in prayer,
But God seems much closer and needed much more
       when trouble and sorrow stand outside our
       door.
For then we seek shelter in His wondrous love
       and we ask Him to send us help from above.
And that is the reason we know it is true
       that bright, shining hours and dark, sad
       ones, too,
Are part of the plan God made for each one,
       And all we can pray is, "Thy will be done!"

The Heavenly Staircase

Prayers are the stairs that lead to God,
And there's joy every step of the way
When we make our pilgrimage to Him
With love in our hearts each day.

Nothing Is Lost Forever

The waking earth at springtime
   Reminds us it is true
That nothing ever really dies
   That is not born anew.

So trust God's all-wise wisdom
   And doubt the Father never,
For in His heavenly Kingdom
   There is nothing lost forever!

The Better You Know Him

The better you know God, the better you feel,
For to learn more about Him and discover He's real
Can wholly, completely, and miraculously change,
Reshape and remake and then rearrange
Your mixed-up, miserable, and unhappy life
Adrift on the sea of sin-sickened strife.
But when you once know this Man of goodwill,
He will calm your life and say, "Peace, be still."
So open your heart's door and let Christ come in
And He'll give you new life and free you from sin.
For there is no joy that can ever compare
With the joy of knowing you're in God's care.

Try It! It Works!

Stop wishing for things
      you complain you have not
And start making the *best*
      of all that you've got.

The House of Prayer

The house of prayer is no farther away
Than the quiet spot where you kneel and pray,
For the heart is a temple when God is there
As you place yourself in His loving care.

It's Not Enough

It's not enough to say, "I believe,"
It's not enough to ask and receive,
It's not enough to repeat the Lord's Prayer,
It's not enough to just say, "I care,"
It's not enough to be pleasant and kind,
It's not enough to keep God in your mind,
It's not enough just to feed the poor,
It's not enough to forbear and endure,
For while these things are all good to do
They cannot ensure salvation for you,
For not until you are born anew
Can the spirit of God be alive in you.

There's Peace and Calm in the Twenty-third Psalm

With the Lord as your Shepherd
      you have all that you need,
For, if you follow in His footsteps
      wherever He may lead,
He will guard and guide and keep you
      in His loving, watchful care
And, when traveling in dark valleys,
      Your Shepherd will be there.
His goodness is unfailing,
      His kindness knows no end,
For the Lord is a Good Shepherd
      on whom you can depend.
So, when your heart is troubled,
      you'll find peace and calm
If you open up the Bible
      and just read this treasured Psalm.

Begin Each Day by Kneeling to Pray

Start every day
    with a good morning prayer
And God will bless each thing you do
    and keep you in His care.

And never, never, sever
    the Spirit's silken strand
That our Father up in heaven
    holds in His mighty hand!

My Garden of Prayer

My garden beautifies my yard
      and adds fragrance to the air,
But it is also my cathedral
      and my quiet place of prayer.

So little do we realize
      that the glory and the power
Of He who made the universe
      lies hidden in a flower.

Finding Faith in a Flower

Sometimes when faith is running low
And I cannot fathom why things are so,
I walk alone among the flowers I grow
And learn the answers to all I would know.

For among my flowers I have come to see
Life's miracle and its mystery
And standing in silence and reverie
My faith comes flooding back to me!

The Answer

The Answer

In the tiny petal
     of a tiny flower
          that grew from a tiny pod
Is the miracle
     and the mystery
          of all creation and God!

Learn to Rest

We all need short vacations
 in life's fast and maddening race,
An interlude of quietness
 from the constant, jet-age pace.
So, when your day is pressure-packed
 and your hours are all too few,
Just close your eyes and meditate
 and let God talk to you.
For when we keep on pushing,
 we're not following in God's way,
We are foolish, selfish robots
 mechanized to fill each day
With unimportant trivia
 that makes life more complex
And gives us greater problems
 to irritate and vex.
So, when your nervous network
 becomes a tangled mess,
Just close your eyes in silent prayer
 and ask the Lord to bless
Each thought that you are thinking,
 each decision you must make,
As well as every word you speak
 and every step you take.
For only by the grace of God
 can we gain self-control
And only meditative thoughts
 can restore your peace of soul.

Daily Prayers
Dissolve Your Cares

I meet God in the morning
And go with Him through the day,
Then in the stillness of the night
Before sleep comes I pray
That God will just take over
All the problems I couldn't solve
And in the peacefulness of sleep
My cares will all dissolve,

So when I open up my eyes
To greet another day
I'll find myself renewed in strength
And there'll open up a way
To meet what seemed impossible
For me to solve alone
And once again I'll be assured
I am never on my own.

For if we try to stand alone
We are weak and we will fall,
For God is always greatest
When we're helpless, lost, and small.
And no day is unmeetable
If on rising our first thought
Is to thank God for the blessings
That His loving care has brought.

So meet Him in the morning
And go with Him through the day
And thank Him for His guidance
Each evening when you pray,
And if you follow faithfully
This daily way to pray
You will never in your lifetime
Face another hopeless day.

The Best Medication
Is Meditation

If your soul is sick
       and your heart is sad
And the good things in life
       begin to look bad,
Don't be too sure
       that you're physically ill
And run to the doctor
       for a sedative pill.
For nothing can heal
       a soul that is sick
Or guarantee a cure
       as complete and quick
As a heart-to-heart talk
       with God and His Son,
Who on the shore of the Galilee
       just said, "Thy Will be done."
So, when you're feeling downcast,
       seek God in meditation,
For a little talk with Jesus
       is unfailing medication.

Life Can't Always Be a Song . . .

So whenever you are troubled
And everything goes wrong,
It is just God working in you
To make your spirit strong!

Anxious Prayers

When we are deeply disturbed with a problem
And our mind is filled with doubt
And we struggle to find a solution
But there seems to be no way out,

We futilely keep on trying
To untangle our web of distress,
But our own little, puny efforts
Meet with very little success.

And finally exhausted and weary,
Discouraged and downcast and low,
With no foreseeable answer
And with no other place to go,

We kneel down in sheer desperation
And slowly and stumblingly pray,
Then impatiently wait for an answer
Which we fully expect right away.

And then, when God does not answer,
In one, sudden instant we say,
"God does not seem to be listening,
So why should we bother to pray?"

But God can't get through to the anxious
Who are much too impatient to wait,
You have to believe in God's promise
That He comes not too soon or too late,

For, whether God answers promptly
Or delays in answering your prayer,
You must have faith to believe Him
And to know in your heart He'll be there.

So be not impatient or hasty,
Just trust in the Lord and believe,
For whatever you ask in faith and love
In abundance you are sure to receive.

This Is My Prayer

Bless me, heavenly Father,
      forgive my erring ways,
Grant me strength to serve Thee,
      put purpose in my days.
Give me understanding
      enough to make me kind
So I may judge all people
      with my heart and not my mind.
And teach me to be patient
      in everything I do,
Content to trust Your wisdom
      and to follow after You.
And help me when I falter
      and hear me when I pray
And receive me in Thy Kingdom
      to dwell with Thee some day.

Faith Is a Candle

In this sick world of hatred
And violence and sin,
Where men renounce morals
And reject discipline,

We stumble in darkness
Groping vainly for "light"
To distinguish the difference
Between wrong and right,

But dawn cannot follow
This night of despair
Unless faith lights a candle
In all hearts everywhere

And warmed by the glow
Our hate melts away
And love lights the path
To a peaceful, new day.

Make It a
Two-Way Prayer

You're troubled and worried,
      you don't know what to do,
So you seek God in prayer
      and He listens to you,
But you seldom pause
      to let God speak,
You just want the answer
      that you desperately seek.

And after you've pleaded,
      you don't give God a chance
To discuss the best way
      to meet your circumstance
And you really miss
      the best part of prayer
Which is feeling and knowing
      God's presence is there.

For so few of us linger
  to quietly share
The silent communion
  that fills the air
In which God is speaking
  and telling us why
Sometimes there's no answer
  to our immediate cry.

So pause for a while
  and just silently wait
And give God a chance
  to communicate,
For two-way prayer
  forms a joyous relation
When we listen to God
  in shared meditation.

Is Life Worth Living?

The great and small . . . the good and bad,
The young and old . . . the sad and glad
Are asking today, "Is life worth living?"
And the answer is only in loving and giving.
For only love can make man kind
And kindness of heart brings peace of mind.

Widen My Vision

God, open my eyes
        so I may see
And feel Your presence
        close to me.
Give me strength
        for my stumbling feet
As I battle the crowd
        on life's busy street,
And widen the vision
        of my unseeing eyes
So in passing faces
        I'll recognize
Not just a stranger,
        unloved and unknown,
But a friend with a heart
        that is much like my own . . .
Give me perception
        to make me aware
That scattered profusely
        on life's thoroughfare
Are the best gifts of God
        that we daily pass by
As we look at the world
        with an unseeing eye.

Unaware, We Pass Him By

On life's busy thoroughfare
We meet with angels unaware.
But we are too busy to listen or hear,
Too busy to sense that God is near,
Too busy to stop and recognize
The grief that lies in another's eyes,
Too busy to offer to help or share,
Too busy to sympathize or care,
Too busy to do the good things we should,
Telling ourselves we would if we could.
But life is too swift and the pace is too great
And we dare not pause for we might be late
For our next appointment which means so much,
We are willing to brush off the Savior's touch,
And we tell ourselves there will come a day
We will have more time to pause on our way.
But before we know it life's sun has set
And we've passed the Savior but never met,
For hurrying along life's thoroughfare
We passed Him by and remained unaware
That within the very sight of our eye,
Unnoticed, the Son of God passed by.

In Reverent Reverie
God Came to Me

I sat among the people
      in the church of my childhood and youth,
I came back to sing the songs of praise
      and to hear the words of truth.
I looked into the faces
      of the young folks and the old
And listened, as I used to,
      to the sweetest story ever told.
I had come back home to visit
      and to meet friends in glad reunion . . .
But the Sunday that I went to church
      turned out to be communion,
And so it was, when I arose
      from my communion prayer
I no longer saw just faces,
      for God was standing there.

Good Cheer

Quit Supposin'!

If you desire to be happy,
Don't think of the things that you dread—
Just give up supposin' the worst things
And look for the best things instead!

Be of Good Cheer

Since fear and dread and worry
Cannot help in any way,
It's much healthier and happier
To be cheerful every day.

And if we'll only try it
We will find, without a doubt,
A cheerful attitude's something
No one should be without.

For when the heart is cheerful
It cannot be filled with fear,
And without fear the way ahead
Seems more distinct and clear.

And we realize there's nothing
We need ever face alone,
For our heavenly Father loves us
And our problems are His own.

The Joy of
Unselfish Giving

Time is not measured
        by the years that you live
But by the deeds that you do
        and the joy that you give.
And each day as it comes
        brings a chance to each one
To love to the fullest,
        leaving nothing undone
That would brighten the life
        or lighten the load
Of some weary traveler
        lost on life's road.
So what does it matter
        how long we may live
If as long as we live
        we unselfishly give?

How to Find Happiness

Happiness is something that is never far away,
It's as close as the things we do and we say.
So start out today with a smile on your face
And make this world a happier place.

The Key to Living

Let us give ourselves away
Not just today but every day.
And remember a kind and thoughtful deed
Or a hand outstretched in time of need
Is the rarest of gifts, for it is a part
Not of the purse but a loving heart.
And he who gives of himself will find
True joy of heart and peace of mind.

It's Such a Busy World!

Our days are so crowded
        and our hours are so few
And there's so little time
        and so much to do
That the days fly by
        and are over and done
Before we have even
        half begun
To do the things
        that we meant to do
But never have time
        to carry through
And how nice it would be
        if we stopped to say
The things we feel
        in our hearts each day!

Take Time to Be Kind

Kindness is a virtue
      given by the Lord,
It pays dividends in happiness
      and joy is its reward.
For, if you practice kindness
      in all you say and do,
The Lord will wrap His kindness
      around your heart and you,
And wrapped within His kindness
      you are sheltered and secure
And under His direction
      your way is safe and sure.

Happy Returns

The more of everything you share,
The more you'll always have to spare,
For only what you give away
Enriches you from day to day!

What Is Love?

What is love?
No words can define it,
It's something so great
Only God could design it.

Wonder of wonders,
Beyond man's conception,
And only in God
Can love find true perfection,

For love is enduring
And patient and kind,
It judges all things
With the heart not the mind,

And love can transform
The most commonplace
Into beauty and splendor
And sweetness and grace.

For love is unselfish,
Giving more than it takes,
And no matter what happens
Love never forsakes.

It's faithful and trusting
And always believing,
Guileless and honest
And never deceiving.

Yes, love is beyond
What man can define,
For love is immortal
And God's gift is divine!

The Language of the Heart

Just like a sunbeam brightens the sky,
A smile on the face of a passerby
Can make a drab and crowded street
A pleasant place where two smiles meet.

"Love One Another"

"Love one another as I have loved you"
May seem impossible to do,
But if you will try to trust and believe
Great are the joys that you will receive.

For love makes us patient, understanding, and kind,
And we judge with our hearts and not with our mind.

For as soon as love enters the heart's open door,
The faults we once saw are not there anymore,
And the things that seemed wrong begin to look right
When viewed in the softness of love's gentle light.

For love works in ways that are wondrous and strange,
And there is nothing in life that love cannot change,
And all that God promised will someday come true
When you love one another the way He loves you.

The Flower of Friendship

Life is like a garden
And friendship like a flower
That blooms and grows in beauty
With the sunshine and the shower.

And lovely are the blossoms
That are tended with great care
By those who work unselfishly
To make the place more fair.

And, like the garden blossoms,
Friendship's flower grows more sweet
When watched and tended carefully
By those we know and meet.

And, as sunshine adds new fragrance
And raindrops play their part,
Joy and sadness add new beauty
When there's friendship in the heart.

And, if the seed of friendship
Is planted deep and true
And watched with understanding,
Friendship's flower will bloom for you.

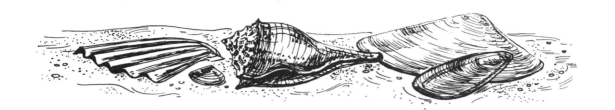

In His Footsteps

When someone does a kindness
          It always seems to me
That's the way God up in heaven
          Would like us all to be.
For when we bring some pleasure
          To another human heart,
We have followed in His footsteps
          And we've had a little part
In serving Him who loves us,
          For I am very sure it's true
That in serving those around us
          We serve and please Him, too.

A Prayer for
Those We Love

"Our Father who art in heaven,"
Hear this little prayer
And reach across the miles today
That stretch from here to there,
So I may feel much closer
To those I'm fondest of
And they may know I think of them
With thankfulness and love.
And help all people everywhere
Who must often dwell apart
To know that they're together
In the haven of the heart!

The Meaning of
True Love

It is sharing and caring,
Giving and forgiving,
Loving and being loved,
Walking hand in hand,
Talking heart to heart,
Seeing through each other's eyes,
Laughing together,
Weeping together,
Praying together,
And always trusting
And believing
And thanking God
For each other.
For love that is shared
is a beautiful thing—
It enriches the soul
and makes the heart sing!

The Gift of Lasting Love

Love is much more than a tender caress
    and more than bright hours of sheer
    happiness,
For a lasting love is made up of sharing
    both hours that are joyous and also
    despairing.
It's made up of patience and deep understanding
    and never of selfish and stubborn demand-
    ing,
It's made up of climbing the steep hills together
    and facing with courage life's stormiest
    weather,
And nothing on earth or heaven can part
    a love that has grown to be part of the heart.
And just like the sun and the stars and the sea,
    this love will go on through eternity,
For true love lives on when earthly things die,
    for it's part of the spirit that soars to the sky.

My Love for You

There are things we cannot measure,
Like the depths of waves and sea
And the heights of stars in heaven
And the joy You bring to me.

Like eternity's long endlessness
And the sunset's golden hue,
There is no way to measure
The love I have for You.

Each Day Brings a Chance to Do Better

God of Creation
Save Our Nation

Great God the Father of all creation,
　　　Look down upon this strife-torn nation,
Revive our spirits lain dormant so long,
　　　Renew our faith and keep it strong,
Forgive our arrogance and greed
　　　And guide us in this hour of need.

Hand of God reach out once more
　　　And with the breath of life restore
Your Spirit in the flesh of men
　　　So we may live in peace again.
For mankind's future and survival
　　　Depend alone on the Spirit's revival!

What Will You Do With This Day?

As we start a new day
      untouched and unmarred,
Unblemished and flawless,
      unscathed and unscarred,
May we try to do better
      and accomplish much more
And be kinder and wiser
      than in the day gone before.
Let us wipe our slates clean
      and start over again,
For God gives this privilege
      to all sincere men
Who will humbly admit
      they have failed many ways
But are willing to try
      and improve these new days
By asking God's help
      in all that they do
And counting on Him
      to refresh and renew
Their courage and faith
      when things go wrong
And the way seems dark
      and the road rough and long.
What will you do
      with this day that's so new?
The choice is yours—
      God leaves that to *you!*

Under New Management

Nothing goes right,
   everything's wrong,
You stumble and fall
   as you trudge along,
The other guy wins,
   but you always lose,
Whatever you hear
   is always bad news.
Well, here's some advice
   that's worth a try,
Businessmen use it
   when they want a new high.
So old management goes
   and the new comes in,
For this is the way
   big business can win.
So if you are trying
   to manage your life,

Yet all around
        is chaos and strife,
Make up your mind
        that you, too, need a change
And start making plans
        to somehow rearrange
The way that you think
        and the things that you do
And what are the things
        that are hindering you.
Then put yourself under
        God's management now,
And when He takes over
        you'll find that somehow
Everything changes,
        Old things pass away,
And the darkness of night
        becomes the brightness of day.
For God can transform
        and change into winners
The losers, and skeptics
        and even the sinners!

Each Day Brings a Chance to Do Better

How often we wish for another chance
      to make a fresh beginning,
A chance to blot out our mistakes
      and change failure into winning.
And it does not take a special time
      to make a brand-new start,
It only takes the deep desire
      to try with all our heart
To live a little better
      and to always be forgiving
And to add a little sunshine
      to the world in which we're living.
So never give up in despair
      and think that you are through,
For there's always a tomorrow
      and a chance to start anew.

Give and Forgive!

Since God forgives us,
        we, too, must forgive
And resolve to do better
        each day that we live
By constantly trying
        to be like Him more nearly
And to trust in His wisdom
        and love Him more dearly.

How to Find
Peace of Mind

We listen to the newscasts
    that come daily to our ears,
We read alarming headlines
    that intensify our fears,
We grow more and more dissatisfied
    and feel less and less secure
As our days become more anxious
    and the future more unsure.
For with violence and dissension
    and chaos all around
We no longer feel with certainty
    that we stand on solid ground.
But in place of reading headlines
    that disturb our peace of mind
We should once more read the Bible
    and on its pages we would find

That this age is no different
       from the millions gone before
And that in every hour of crisis
       God has opened up a door
To all who seek His guidance
       and trust His all-wise plan,
For God provides protection
       beyond that devised by man,
And while God's almighty power
       is not ours to understand,
We know who holds the future
       and we know who holds our hand.
And to have the steadfast knowledge
       that we never walk alone
And to rest in the assurance
       that our every need is known
Will help dispel our worries
       and in trusting Him we'll find
Right in the midst of chaos
       God can give us peace of mind!

Show Me More Clearly

God, help me in my feeble way
To somehow do something each day
To show You that I love You best
And that my faith will stand each test
And let me serve You every day
And feel You near me when I pray.
Oh, hear my prayer, dear God above,
And make me worthy of Your love!

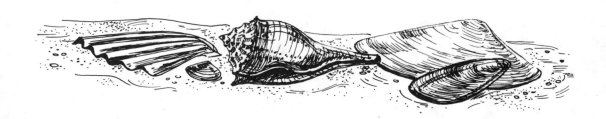

The Golden Years of Life

God in His loving
      and all-wise way
Makes the heart
      that was once young and gay
Serene and more gentle
      and less restless, too,
Content to remember
      the joys it once knew.

And all that we sought
      on the pathway of pleasure
Becomes but a memory
      to cherish and treasure.
The fast pace grows slower
      and the spirit serene,
And our souls can envision
      what our eyes have not seen.

And so while life's springtime
      is sweet to recall,
The autumn of life
      is the best time of all,
For our wild, youthful yearnings
      all gradually cease
And God fills our days
      with beauty and peace!

A Prayer of Thanks

Thank You, God, for everything
  I've experienced here on earth,
Thank You for protecting me
  from the moment of my birth,
And thank You for the beauty
  around me everywhere,
The gentle rain and glistening dew,
  the sunshine and the air,
The joyous gift of feeling
  the soul's soft, whispering voice
That speaks to me from deep within
  and makes my heart rejoice.
O God, no words are great enough
  to thank You just for living,
And that is why every day
  is a day for real thanksgiving.

Inspiration!
Meditation!

Brighten your day
And lighten your way,
Lessen your cares
With daily prayers,
Quiet your mind
And leave tension behind
And find inspiration
In hushed meditation.

This Is All I Ask

Lord, show me the way
I can somehow repay
The blessings You've given to me.

Lord, teach me to do
What You most want me to
And to be what You want me to be.

I'm unworthy I know
But I do love You so,
I beg You to answer my plea.

I've not much to give
But as long as I live
May I give it completely to Thee!